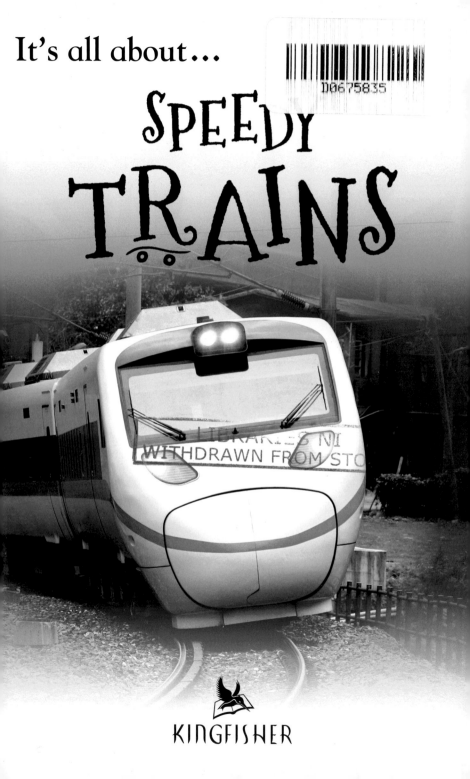

It's all about…

SPEEDY TRAINS

KINGFISHER

KINGFISHER

First published 2016 by Kingfisher
an imprint of Macmillan Children's Books
20 New Wharf Road, London N1 9RR
Associated companies throughout the world
www.panmacmillan.com

Series editor: Sarah Snashall
Series design: Anthony Hannant (LittleRedAnt)
Adapted from an original text by Thea Feldman

ISBN 978-0-7534-3941-8

9 8 7 6 5 4 3 2 1

1TR/1115/WKT/UG/128MA

A CIP catalogue record for this book is available from the British Library.

Printed in China

Picture credits
The Publisher would like to thank the following for permission to reproduce their material.
Top = t; Bottom = b; Centre = c; Left = l; Right = r;
Cover Shutterstock/topimages; Back cover, Pages 2–3, 30–31 Shutterstock/Vincent St Thomas;
Page 5t Alamy/Chromomorange/Manfred Dietsch; 6–7 Alamy/Keasbury-Gordon Photograph Collection;
7t Getty/Time Life Pictures; 8–9 Alamy/Classicstock; 8b Alamy/Photos12 Collection; 9t Alamy/
ArtArchive; 10b Getty/Heritage Images/Hulton Fine Art Collection; 10–11 Alamy/B Lawrence;
12b, 25c Shutterstock/serjio74; 12–13 Flickr/Matt Buck; 13t Getty/Central press/Hulton Archive;
14–15 Shutterstock/Aleksandr Riutin; 15t Flickr/Brandy; 15b Shutterstock/huyangshu;
16–17 Shutterstock/Viacheslav Lopatin; 16b Shutterstock/Manfred Steinbach; 17c Shutterstock/
katatonia82; 18 Getty/SSPL/Manchester Daily Express; 19 Flickr/Simon Pielow; 19t Getty/Gallo Image
Lanz von Horsten; 20 Shutterstock/Matthew Siddons; 21t Shutterstock/trubityn; 21b Shutterstock/
antb; 22 Shutterstock/cyo bo; 23 Alamy/epa european pressphoto agency bv; 23t Shutterstock/ Leonid
Andronov; 24 Getty/SSPL; 25 Flickr/News Oresund; 26 Shutterstock/Martin M303; 27t Alamy/AF Archiv
27b Shutterstock/Ron Ellis; 28 Flickr/scjody; 29 Shutterstock/Kijja Pruchyathamkorn; 29t Shutterstoc
hanmon; 32 Dreamstime/Sébastien Bonaimé.
Cards: Front tl Shutterstock/Wayne0216; tr Shutterstock/Meoita; bl Alamy/B Lawrence; Back tl Flickr
maxintosh; tr Flickr/Jim; bl, Alamy/epa european pressphoto agency bv; br Flickr/Simon Pielow.

Front cover: The *Taroko Express*, a tilting express train, speeds through Taiwan.

CONTENTS

All kinds of train

A train is a vehicle that runs on rails. A train set is made up of a locomotive that pulls a number of carriages or cars. There are passenger trains, goods trains, luxury trains, underground trains – and toy trains!

FACT...

A wagonway was used in Greece in about 600BCE to move boats across a small stretch of land.

Is it a boat? Is it a train? This train moves boats from one canal to another in Poland.

SPOTLIGHT: Bullet train O series

Famous for:	first high-speed train
Built for:	Tokaido–Shinkansen line, Japan
Built:	1964
Top speed:	210 km/h

From cart to train

On 21 February, 1804 a steam
engine pulled a train along rails at
an ironworks in Wales. The railway
age had begun. Twenty years later,
George Stephenson opened the first
passenger train line: the Stockton and
Darlington railway.

**Robert Stephenson's design for the *Rocket*
was used for future steam engines.**

Famous for: ground-breaking steam train

Designed by: Robert Stephenson

Built: 1829

Top speed: 45 km/h

FACT...

William Huskisson, the Member of Parliament for Liverpool, was hit and killed by the *Rocket* at the opening ceremony of the Liverpool and Manchester Railway in 1830.

The first passenger carriage looked like a road coach.

7

Railways everywhere

Soon great projects built railways across the world. Thousands and thousands of workers built the railways by hand. It was dangerous and hard work.

Labourers working on the New York Central Railroad.

Three workers died for every kilometre of track built on the East African Railway.

British engineers travelled around the world building railways.

FACT...

In 1830 there were 157 kilometres of train track in Britain. By 1860 there were 16,790 kilometres.

The age of steam

Over the next 100 years trains became the most popular form of long-distance transport for goods and passengers. Trains became faster and faster. In the 1930s, Sir Nigel Gresley built two record-breaking streamlined trains: the *Flying Scotsman* and *Mallard*.

SPEED TO THE WEST
GWR
GWR
CORNWALL DEVON SOMERSET WALES

Trains soon became the fastest way to travel long distances.

Famous for:	fastest steam train
Designed by:	Sir Nigel Gresley
Built:	1938
Top speed:	201 km/h

Mallard is still the fastest-ever steam train.

MALLARD

Nº 446

Diesel, electric – and jet!

The first trains were steam trains – huge coal fires heated water to make steam to move the engine. Later there were powerful diesel trains and fast electric trains. A few trains have even been built with jet engines.

FACT...

The first diesel engine was designed by Dr Rudolf Diesel.

Electric trains use electricity from overhead wires.

Turbo trains could travel at 250 kilometres an hour.

SPOTLIGHT: Intercity 125

Famous for:	fastest diesel train in the world
Used by:	British Rail
First used:	1976
Top speed:	238 km/h

Great rail journeys

The first train journey was 40 kilometres long. Today you can travel for thousands of miles across continents without changing trains. Passengers can eat in special dining carriages and can sleep in proper beds.

The Trans-Siberian Railway travels across a third of the world in five and a half days.

Russia – China: Moscow to Beijing (Trans-Siberian Railway)	7826 km
Canada: Toronto to Vancouver	4466 km
Australia: Sydney to Perth	4352 km
India: Dibrugarh to Kanyakumari	4238 km

It takes three and a half days to travel from Toronto to Vancouver in Canada.

It takes two days to travel from Shanghai (China) to Lhasa (Tibet, China).

Going underground

If you go to London, Paris, New York or Shanghai there will be trains rumbling deep beneath your feet. There are 148 cities in the world with underground trains. The Shanghai Metro in China has the most track, the New York Metro has the most stations and the Kiev Metro in the Ukraine is the deepest.

Komsomolskaya metro station in Moscow, Russia, looks like a palace.

Station in Munich, Germany

FACT...

Arsenalna Station on the Kiev Metro in the Ukraine is 105 metres below ground and is the deepest station in the world.

A tram is a small electric train that runs on rails in cities.

Luxury trains

Have you ever had to stand up on a packed train? Well, next time you travel, why don't you pick something more luxurious? Passengers can travel in style on the *Orient Express* across Europe, the *Blue Train* across South Africa or the *Maharajas' Express* across India.

The *Orient Express*, the world's first luxury train, ran from Paris, France to Istanbul in Turkey.

FACT...

Suites on board South Africa's *Blue Train* come with their own personal butler.

the *Blue Train*

The *Maharajas' Express* has two restaurants, a bar, a library and a Presidential suite.

Working hard

Most of the world's goods are moved by train. Goods trains can have up to 100 goods wagons and can be seven kilometres long. Long goods trains sometimes have two or three locomotives pulling them.

Containers of goods can be double stacked on long trains.

Goods trains can move heavy items such as tankers or open wagons full of coal or rocks.

FACT...

A fully laden goods train can take one kilometre to stop.

A snow blower is used to clear snowy tracks in Canada.

Fastest trains

High-speed trains travel at top speeds on special electric lines. The trains have sleek shapes to cut through the air. The fastest trains today are held 10 centimetres above the rails by magnets.

Spotlight: Shanghai Maglev

Famous for:	fastest scheduled train
First used:	2004
Average speed:	251 km/h
Top speed:	430 km/h

The *TGV* is France's high-speed train.

World speed records

Conventional train in test: TGV – 575 km/h (2007)

Non-conventional train in test:
L0 Series Maglev – 603 km/h (2015)

Scheduled train: Shanghai Maglev – 430 km/h

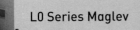

L0 Series Maglev

Tunnels and bridges

Trains are not very good at going up or down steep hills. Bridges and tunnels are built to help keep the track flat and to cross rivers and roads.

Enormous tunnel-boring machines were used to dig the 50-kilometre-long Channel Tunnel.

FACT...

The longest rail bridge in the world is the Danyang–Kunshun Bridge in China. It is 165 kilometres long and took 10,000 people four years to build.

The Landwasser viaduct in Switzerland goes into a tunnel in the cliff face.

The bridge and tunnel that connect Sweden and Denmark meet at an artificial island.

Trains in films

Some of the most famous trains of all time only exist in books and films: the *Hogwarts Express*, Thomas the Tank Engine and the *Polar Express*.

The *Hogwarts Express* crossed the Glenfinnan viaduct in Scotland.

The *Polar Express* took children to see Father Christmas.

FACT...

Reverend Richard Awdry created the story of Thomas the Tank Engine to cheer up his son Christopher while he had measles.

Unlike the other engines, Thomas carries his own water (in a tank) and coal.

Highest, longest, cutest

Every day 20 million people travel on Indian railways. Here are some more amazing train numbers.

Longest railway: Moscow to Vladivostock 9259 kilometres

Highest railway: Tanggula Pass, Tibet, China 5072 metres

Longest passenger train: Ringling Bros. and Barnum & Bailey Circus trains - 1.6 kilometres

Busiest train station: Shinjuko Station, Tokyo, Japan – 1.26 million passengers a day

The cutest train? Japanese train *Tama Densha* is covered in pictures of the railway cat.

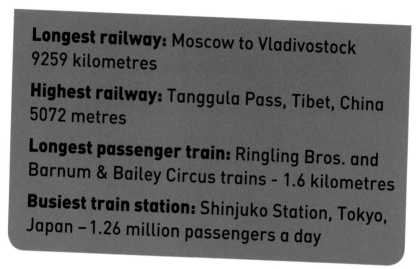

The Gornergrat rack railway in Switzerland is the highest open-air railway in Europe.

When there is no room inside the train, people are allowed to travel on the roof in India.

वातानुकूलित 2-टियर शयनयान
AC TWO TIER SLEEPER

29

GLOSSARY

bullet train The nickname of the *Shinkansen*, a high-speed passenger train in Japan.

butler A servant that looks after you.

canal A river that has been built by people. Boats can travel along it.

container A large metal box that you can put things into.

diesel train A train with an engine that runs on diesel fuel.

electric train A train that runs on electricity from overhead cables.

goods train A train that carries materials, heavy loads and other things, but not passengers.

high-speed train A fast train that runs on its own special track.

ironworks A place where iron is made.

locomotive A railway engine that pulls railway wagons.

luxury train A train with the most comfortable carriages.

Maglev A train that is held above the rails by magnets.

snow blower A train that clears snow off rail tracks.

steam train A train that uses steam to move.

suite A group of rooms.

turbo train A train that is powered by a jet engine.

underground train A train that runs through tunnels underneath big cities.

viaduct A bridge over a valley.

wagonway A simple rail track for wagons.

INDEX

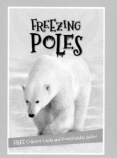

BEASTLY BUGS

FREE Collector Cards and Downloadable Audio!

DEADLY DINOSAURS

FREE Collector Cards and Downloadable Audio!

FANTASTIC FLIERS

FREE Collector Cards and Downloadable Audio!

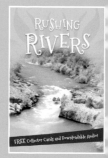

FAST CARS

FREE Collector Cards and Downloadable Audio!

FREEZING POLES

FREE Collector Cards and Downloadable Audio!

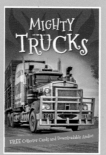

MIGHTY TRUCKS

FREE Collector Cards and Downloadable Audio!

RIOTOUS RAINFORESTS

FREE Collector Cards and Downloadable Audio!

RUSHING RIVERS

FREE Collector Cards and Downloadable Audio!